SUPREME MISCONDUCT

THE ROAD TRIPS OF JUSTICE TUCKER

CHUCK SHAPIRO

CONTENTS

FOREWORD

Foreword by Dick Gibson

As I sat down to write this foreword for Chuck Shapiro's "Supreme Misconduct: The Road Trips of Justice Tucker," I couldn't help but reflect on the intricate dance between fiction and reality. Shapiro's novel, a satirical odyssey into the heart of American jurisprudence, is a reminder of how closely the absurdities of fiction can mirror the complexities of real life.

I have known Chuck for many years. His keen observations of the legal world, coupled with a sharp wit, have always made for engaging and insightful conversations. When he first mentioned his project, I was immediately intrigued. The result, as you will soon discover, is nothing short of a literary roller coaster.

"Supreme Misconduct" is a bold exploration of the American legal system through the eyes of Justice Cedric Tucker, a character whose antics and rulings from his roving

RV courtroom challenge the traditional tenets of law and justice.

This novel does what great satire should do – it entertains, it provokes, and it questions. It invites us to look at the legal system and those who operate within it through a lens that is at once critical and comical. Shapiro masterfully uses humor to dissect complex legal and ethical issues, making them accessible and engaging. In doing so, he not only entertains but also illuminates the oft-overlooked human element in the machinery of justice.

As you turn the pages, you will be drawn into a world where the line between right and wrong, legal and ethical, is blurred. You will find yourself laughing, pondering, and perhaps even questioning the very foundations of justice and morality. And that, I believe, is the mark of a truly impactful work of fiction.

In "Supreme Misconduct," Chuck Shapiro has crafted a story that is as thought-provoking as it is entertaining. It is a testament to his talent and his deep understanding of the legal landscape. So, without further ado, I invite you to delve into the world of Justice Cedric Tucker – a journey that promises to be as enlightening as it is enjoyable.

Dick Gibson

PART I

THE RISE OF CEDRIC TUCKER

1

THE CORONATION OF JUSTICE TUCKER

In the hallowed and usually solemn chambers of the United States Supreme Court, a peculiar air of expectancy hung thick. It was not every day that a vacancy on the Supreme Court was filled, let alone by someone as... uniquely controversial as Judge Cedric Tucker.

The retirement of the first-ever African-American justice had left a gap that President Roth, known for his shrewd, if not always popular, decisions, was eager to fill.

"WHAT A NICE MATCH," President Roth had declared with a grin that spoke of political games well-played, upon nominating Tucker. It was, after all, a clever stroke - appointing a conservative justice born in Georgia, a man who, like his predecessor, shared the same skin color but stood on the completely opposite end of the ideological spectrum.

THE CEREMONY WAS anything but understated. The grandiose room echoed with the murmur of distinguished guests - politicians, esteemed lawyers, and of course, Tucker's family.

They whispered about Tucker's notorious rulings from his short stint as an appellate judge, his fondness for driving his RV across the states, and his radical interpretations of the Constitution that had both bewildered and endeared him to many.

As TUCKER STEPPED IN, resplendent in his new robe, which seemed to have been tailored to add an extra flair of authority, a hush fell over the crowd.

His wife, Jinny, a vision of supportive poise, was by his side, her smile a perfect curve of political correctness.

THE IRONY of the moment was not lost on the attendees. Here was Cedric Tucker, about to be sworn in as a guardian of the Constitution, a man whose relationship with the said Constitution was akin to a chef with a penchant for rewriting recipes - sometimes with brilliant results and other times with disastrous concoctions.

CHIEF JUSTICE RANDALL, an old hawk in the legal realm, administered the oath with a tone that suggested he was simultaneously performing a sacred ritual and opening Pandora's box.

Tucker's voice was steady as he recited the oath, his eyes gleaming with a cocktail of pride, ambition, and a hint of defiance.

· · ·

As he uttered the final words, "So help me God," a murmur rippled through the room.

It was a mixture of awe, skepticism, and for some, a thinly veiled dread of what was to come.

President Roth's expression, however, was one of unadulterated triumph.

In Tucker, he had found not just a justice, but a chess piece in the grand political game - a conservative black judge from Georgia, no less.

"What a nice match," he had said. Indeed, in the game of politics, it was a masterstroke.

The ceremony concluded with a flourish, and as the room emptied, the air seemed charged with questions about the future.

What kind of justice would Cedric Tucker turn out to be? Would he uphold the sanctity of the law, or would he rewrite it in his own image, or worse?

Only time would tell. But for now, the stage was set for the most unconventional Justice the Supreme Court had ever seen. The coronation of Justice Tucker was complete, and the wheels of change, or perhaps of chaos, had begun to turn.

2

JUDGMENTS ON THE JOURNEY

A s the sun rose over the nation's capital, casting a golden glow on the marble edifice of the Supreme Court, Justice Cedric Tucker was already miles away, both in distance and thought. For him, the courtroom was wherever his RV was parked – a notion that both bemused and alarmed the legal community.

HIS RV, affectionately nicknamed 'The Court Cruiser' by some and 'The Roaming Bench' by others less fond of him, was parked at his home near the Court.

Here, surrounded by nature's serenity, Tucker believed he found clarity of thought that the traditional chambers could never afford him.

INSIDE THE RV, the setting was a strange blend of a judge's chamber and a comfortable living room.

One side of the vehicle was lined with law books, their spines showing signs of frequent use. The other side boasted a cozy seating area, complete with plush sofas and a small coffee table, on which rested a pile of legal briefs and a half-drunk cup of coffee.

TUCKER SAT AT A MAKESHIFT DESK – a fold-out table really – peering over his glasses at a contentious case file. The case in question revolved around a complex environmental regulation dispute, but Tucker's mind was not on the legal intricacies.

He was mulling over the broader implications, how his decision could be a landmark in asserting property rights over environmental concerns.

AS HE MADE NOTES, his phone buzzed – a text from Jinny, checking in on him. "Don't forget to eat something healthy," it read.

Tucker smiled and typed a quick reply, assuring her he had fruit, conveniently omitting the bacon sandwich he'd devoured earlier.

THE IRONY OF JUSTICE TUCKER, a man entrusted with upholding the Constitution, operating out of a vehicle often used for family vacations, was not lost on his critics. His supporters, however, saw it as a sign of the Justice being authentic and down-to-earth.

LATER THAT DAY, as Tucker convened a video conference with his clerks, the backdrop of his RV interior juxtaposed with their formal attire created an almost comical scene.

He discussed the case with surprising rigor, his radical viewpoints clashing with the more conventional stances of his younger clerks.

The debate was lively, but his younger clerks seemed intimidated by him, partly to do with the accusations against him prior to his appointment.

AS THE MEETING CONCLUDED, Tucker leaned back in his chair, a satisfied grin on his face. This was his domain, his court on wheels, where the rules were his to make, and justice was, quite literally, a journey.

THE DAY DREW to a close with Tucker sitting by a small campfire outside the RV, case files on his lap, under a sky full of stars. In this tranquil solitude, he was more than a justice; he was a philosopher-king of his own nomadic realm, charting a course through the legal wilderness.

But as the flames flickered, casting long shadows, they seemed to dance with the questions and controversies that followed him.

3

ARMS AND THE MAN

J ustice Cedric Tucker sat in his RV, the Court Cruiser, a mug of coffee in hand, staring contemplatively at the case file in front of him.

The case was a heated Second Amendment dispute, one that had the nation's attention.

Tucker, known for his unconventional interpretations of the Constitution, saw this as more than a legal challenge; it was an opportunity to imprint his unique judicial philosophy on the annals of American law.

THE RV WAS PARKED in a secluded corner of a national park in Virginia, far from the distractions of Washington.

Tucker preferred the solitude when contemplating cases of such magnitude. It gave him the space to think, to dissect the legal arguments without the incessant buzz of the capital.

. . .

As he sifted through the amicus briefs, Tucker's mind wandered to his own upbringing in Georgia.

He remembered the hunting trips with his father, the early lessons in handling firearms, and the sense of responsibility and freedom they instilled. Those memories shaped his views on gun rights, views that were often at odds with the prevailing sentiments in the Supreme Court.

Tucker chuckled to himself, thinking about how his colleagues would react to his impending opinion.

He imagined their furrowed brows and the polite yet pointed debates that would ensue.

They viewed the Second Amendment through a narrow, almost academic lens, he thought. For Tucker, it was about tradition, heritage, and a fundamental right that was as much a part of America as the Constitution itself.

As he penned his thoughts, Tucker's reasoning was bold, even radical. He argued that the Second Amendment wasn't just about the right to bear arms but was a cornerstone of American identity.

His draft opinion included references to historical militias, the importance of self-defense in the early colonies, and the role of firearms in shaping the nation.

Tucker knew his stance was provocative, but he was not shy of fueling the flames of the already heated national debate on gun control.

His argument focused on constitutional interpretation,

on what he believed the framers intended when they penned the Bill of Rights.

It was a tightrope walk between his personal beliefs and the legal reasoning required of a Supreme Court Justice.

AS THE SUN SET OUTSIDE, casting long shadows across the interior of the RV, Tucker leaned back in his chair. He felt a sense of satisfaction, having laid down an opinion that was true to his beliefs yet mindful of the legal precedents.

It was an opinion that would undoubtedly stir controversy, but Tucker was not one to shy away from it. He believed in the law, in the Constitution, and in a justice system that allowed for diverse interpretations.

CLOSING THE CASE FILE, Tucker stepped outside the RV, taking in the crisp evening air. He looked up at the stars, thinking about the weight of his decisions, the impact they had on the country, and the legacy he was creating.

It was a heavy burden, but one he bore with pride.

Tomorrow, he would send his draft opinion to his clerks for review, but tonight, he was just Cedric Tucker, a man with his thoughts and the vast, open sky.

4

LIBERTIES AND LIBERTIES

T he early morning light filtered through the blinds of Justice Tucker's RV, casting long, narrow shadows across the interior. Cedric Tucker sat at his desk, surrounded by legal tomes and papers, deeply engrossed in the case that lay open before him.

This was no ordinary case; it pertained to the Fourteenth Amendment, a cornerstone of American civil liberties. Tucker, with his characteristic blend of reverence and audacity towards the Constitution, was ready to tackle it head-on.

THIS CASE WAS a complex puzzle of civil rights, touching upon issues of equality and state power. Tucker's views on the Fourteenth Amendment were well-known for their unorthodoxy, often leaning towards interpretations that favored states' rights, even when they seemed to be at odds with contemporary understandings of civil liberties.

As a African-American conservative judge from the South, his perspectives were shaped by a unique blend of personal history, judicial philosophy, and a deep-seated belief in the original intent of the Constitution's framers.

TUCKER'S APPROACH to this case was considered meticulous by himself and his friend, a fellow Justice on the bench who had the nickname, Timo.

He poured over historical documents, past Supreme Court rulings, and scholarly articles, each providing a different lens through which the Fourteenth Amendment could be viewed. His pen moved furiously, jotting down notes, ideas, and arguments.

This was a man who believed in the power of the written word, in the power of legal reasoning to bring about change, even if it was controversial.

AS THE DAY PROGRESSED, the RV became a crucible of legal thought. Tucker paced back and forth, sometimes staring out the window at the tranquil scenery, at other times, burying his head in his hands, deep in thought. The Fourteenth Amendment, with its broad implications for civil rights, was a battleground of interpretation, and Tucker was determined to plant his flag firmly in the ground.

HIS DRAFT OPINION WAS BOLD, to say the least. He argued for a more constrained view of the Amendment, one that would give states greater leeway in determining the balance between individual rights and state interests.

His reasoning was peppered with historical references, pointing to a time when states wielded more power, a time he believed was more in line with the vision of the Constitution's framers.

HOWEVER, Tucker was not insensitive to the potential backlash his opinion might generate. He knew that his stance would be met with criticism, perhaps even outrage, in certain circles. But so what?

He was resolute, driven by a conviction that his interpretation was not only legally sound but necessary for a true understanding of the Fourteenth Amendment, and also, by his ego. "Those liberals are going to suffer as long as I am on the bench."

AS DUSK FELL, Tucker sat back in his chair, his eyes tired but resolute. He knew that the road ahead would be tumultuous, that his opinion would stir a hornet's nest. But as he gazed out at the stars beginning to twinkle in the night sky, he felt a sense of peace.

In his heart, he believed that justice was not about going along with the tide but about standing firm in the face of adversity, about having the courage to speak what one believed to be the truth.

IN THE SOLITUDE of his RV, Justice Cedric Tucker prepared himself for the storm that was to come, armed with nothing but his pen and his convictions.

The liberties he interpreted, much like the road he traveled, were narrow, never open to exploration or new paths, let alone to new understandings.

5

JINNY'S CRUSADE

The sun had just begun to peek through the blinds of their stately home, casting a warm glow over the elegant interior.

Jinny Tucker moved with purpose through the rooms, her mind buzzing with plans and strategies.

Unlike the traditional image of a judge's wife, Jinny was a force unto herself – a political activist known for her fiery spirit and unyielding commitment to her causes.

IN THE KITCHEN, she multitasked with ease, preparing breakfast while scrolling through her tablet, reviewing the latest news and updates from her various advocacy groups.

Her involvement in political activism wasn't just a pastime; it was a passion that ran as deep in her veins as her love for Cedric.

· · ·

JINNY'S RELATIONSHIP with her husband, Justice Cedric Tucker, was a complex tapestry of love, respect, and ideological clashes.

She was well aware of Cedric's unique approach to justice, his controversial rulings, and his maverick status in the legal world.

Rather than shy away from it, Jinny often saw it as an opportunity, a platform from which she could influence change and champion her causes.

THEIR BREAKFAST CONVERSATIONS WERE LIVELY, often turning into spirited debates about legal principles, civil rights, and the role of the judiciary.

This morning was no different. As Cedric joined her at the table, Jinny wasted no time in diving into a heated discussion about a recent environmental case that was making its way through the courts.

"YOU HAVE AN OPPORTUNITY HERE, CEDRIC," Jinny pressed, her eyes alight with fervor. "Your position on this case could set a precedent for environmental protection."

CEDRIC, accustomed to his wife's passionate pleas, sipped his coffee, listening intently.

He admired Jinny's dedication, even if he didn't always agree with her viewpoints.

Their debates were a testament to the strength of their relationship, each challenging the other to think deeper, to consider perspectives beyond their own.

· · ·

JINNY, for her part, was not one to back down easily.

She saw Cedric's role as a Supreme Court Justice as a powerful tool for social change, and she often sought to steer him towards rulings that aligned with her activist agenda.

She believed in the law as a vehicle for justice in the broadest sense, encompassing not just legal justice, but social and environmental justice as well.

AS BREAKFAST CAME TO AN END, Jinny handed Cedric a folder filled with research and articles related to the case. "Just some reading material," she said with a wink. Cedric took it, knowing full well that it was Jinny's way of influencing his thoughts on the matter.

JINNY TUCKER WAS MORE than just a spouse to a Supreme Court Justice; she was a crusader in her own right, a woman who wielded her influence within the halls of power, albeit from the sidelines.

Her dynamic with Cedric was a dance of intellect and wills, a partnership that, while sometimes contentious, was built on a foundation of mutual respect and a shared desire to leave an indelible mark on the world.

AS CEDRIC LEFT for his RV, the mobile bastion of his judicial work, Jinny turned to her own day, filled with meetings and advocacy work.

In their own ways, both were shaping the course of history, their lives intertwined in the pursuit of justice, each according to their own vision.

PART II

THE SHADOW OF TIMO

6

IN TIMO'S SHADOW

As dusk settled over the landscape, painting the sky in hues of orange and purple, Justice Cedric Tucker sat in his RV, enveloped in the quietude that only nature could provide. His thoughts, however, were far from quiet, as they often wandered to the memory of his late colleague and friend, Justice Timo.

JUSTICE TIMO HAD BEEN MORE than just a fellow member of the bench; he was a kindred spirit to Tucker in many ways.

A conservative powerhouse with a sharp legal mind, Timo had often been Tucker's ally in the court's ideological battles.

Yet, the differences in their approaches to jurisprudence were stark and significant, casting Tucker perpetually in Timo's shadow, even posthumously.

TUCKER REFLECTED on their numerous conversations and debates, a ritual that had shaped much of his own judicial philosophy. Timo had been a bastion of traditionalism, often advocating for a stringent interpretation of the Constitution. Tucker, with his more maverick approach, had frequently found himself both challenged and inspired by Timo's steadfast views.

Now, in the solitude of his RV, Tucker often found himself grappling with the legal and ethical dilemmas that had once been the crux of their discussions.

He pondered what Timo would have made of his recent decisions, his unconventional methods, and his seemingly radical interpretations of the law.

Would he have approved, or would he have offered that characteristic mix of stern admonition and wise counsel?

As he delved into his case files, Tucker couldn't shake off the feeling of being in Timo's shadow, of living up to a legacy that was marked by rigorous legal scholarship and unwavering commitment to conservative principles.

Tucker admired Timo's charisma and decisiveness, qualities he sometimes found himself struggling with amidst his own complex, and often controversial, views.

The night deepened, and Tucker sat there, surrounded by the memories of his friend, feeling both the weight of his absence and the influence of his legacy.

It was a complex dance of respect, rivalry, and reflection that continued to shape Tucker's path on the bench.

. . .

IN HIS MOMENTS OF SOLITUDE, Tucker grappled with the shadows Timo left behind – shadows that were both a guiding light and a benchmark against which he measured his own judicial journey.

As he closed another case file, the silence around him felt more profound, a reminder of the solitary path he now tread, a path once walked alongside a friend and a mentor.

THE LEGACY OF JUSTICE TIMO, with its traditionalist undertones and staunch adherence to the letter of the law, lingered in the air.

It was a presence that Tucker both revered and wrestled with, as he carved his own niche in the annals of judicial history.

IN THE QUIET of the night, in the heart of the wilderness, Justice Cedric Tucker sat, contemplating the complex tapestry of his career – one that was intricately interwoven with the enduring shadow of Justice Timo.

7

THE INSECURITY OF A JUSTICE

I n the dim light of early dawn, Justice Cedric Tucker sat in contemplative silence in his RV, the Court Cruiser.

Outside, the world was slowly awakening, but inside the confines of his mobile workspace, Tucker was lost in introspection, grappling with a ghost that had long haunted him – the ghost of perceived inferiority to his late colleague, Justice Timo.

TIMO HAD BEEN a colossus in the legal world, renowned for his intellectual rigor and conservative jurisprudence.

In contrast, Tucker, despite his own accomplishments, often felt relegated to the role of a secondary figure, an echo of Timo's brilliance. The legal community, the media, and even their peers on the bench, it seemed to him, had always viewed Tucker as walking in Timo's shadow, never quite his equal.

.   .   .

THIS PERCEPTION HAD GNAWED at Tucker over the years. He resented the insinuation that his thoughts and rulings were mere reflections of Timo's ideology, that he lacked a unique judicial voice. In the solitude of the RV, these thoughts took on a sharper edge, fueling a determination to prove himself as a jurist of singular merit and vision.

AS HE POURED over case files, Tucker's mind turned to the decisions he had made since Timo's passing. Each one had been bolder than the last, a conscious effort to step out of the shadow cast by his old friend. He had ventured into uncharted legal territories, often courting controversy, driven by a need to assert his intellectual independence.

HIS RULINGS HAD BECOME MORE pronounced, more ideologically driven. He pushed the boundaries of conservative legal thought, often taking positions that even Timo might have hesitated to endorse.

In his quest to establish his identity, Tucker had embraced a radicalism that was as much about proving his detractors wrong as it was about interpreting the law.

THIS MORNING WAS NO DIFFERENT. Tucker was deliberating over a case that presented an opportunity to make a bold statement, a chance to leave an indelible mark on the legal landscape.

The case, which involved a complex intersection of states' rights and federal oversight, was contentious, and Tucker's preliminary thoughts leaned towards a decision that would undoubtedly raise eyebrows and elicit sharp criticism.

YET, as he reviewed his notes, a nagging doubt lingered in the back of his mind. Was he pushing the envelope too far? Was his desire to emerge from Timo's shadow compromising his judicial judgment?

These questions were quickly brushed aside, overshadowed by the burning need to establish his legacy, distinct and distinguished from that of Justice Timo.

AS THE FIRST light of day broke through the windows of the RV, Tucker set his pen to paper, his resolve firm. Today's opinions would be as radical as one could imagine, uninfluenced by the specter of his past associations. They would be bold, they would be drastic, and they would be unmistakably Tucker.

IN THE QUIET of the morning, Justice Cedric Tucker embarked on a path that he hoped would redefine his career. But whether this path would lead to the recognition he craved or to further controversy, only time would tell.

For now, he was a man on a mission, a mission to step out of the long, imposing shadow of Justice Timo.

8

A RADICAL TURN

The sun was high in the sky, casting a warm glow inside Justice Tucker's RV. Amidst the quiet hum of the countryside, Tucker sat at his makeshift desk, papers strewn around him, a look of intense concentration etched on his face. He was on the cusp of making a decision that would not only define his career but also mark a radical shift in his judicial philosophy.

SINCE THE PASSING of Justice Timo, Tucker had felt an overwhelming need to establish himself as a formidable intellect in his own right. He was tired of the comparisons, the insinuations that he was merely a shadow of his late colleague. It was this desire to assert his independence that had led him to take increasingly bold, often controversial stances on key legal issues.

TODAY, Tucker was deliberating on a case that involved environmental regulations versus industrial growth. The case had become a battleground for broader ideological conflicts, pitting environmentalists against big business interests. Tucker's finger hovered over a line he had just written, a line that argued for sweeping deregulation, favoring economic interests over environmental concerns. It was a stance that would shock many, potentially outraging environmental advocates and a significant portion of the public.

TUCKER WAS aware of the implications. His decision would not only affect the immediate case but also set a precedent that could reshape environmental policy nationwide. It was a radical departure from the Court's previous stances, a move that could be seen as judicial activism of the highest order.

AS HE PONDERED over his draft decision, Tucker's mind was a whirlwind of thoughts. He recalled his conversations with Jinny, her passionate advocacy for environmental causes, and how this decision would place him directly at odds with her beliefs. He thought about the legacy of Justice Timo, a man who had always championed judicial restraint and adherence to the letter of the law.

BUT TUCKER WAS UNDETERRED. He saw this as an opportunity to make a bold statement, to carve out a legal legacy that was distinctly his own. He believed that the Court had become too cautious, too restrained, and it was time to take a stand, to shape the law rather than simply interpret it.

With a resolute stroke of his pen, Tucker finalized his decision, setting into motion a series of events that would reverberate through the legal community and beyond. He leaned back in his chair, a sense of accomplishment mixed with apprehension washing over him. He had made his mark, but at what cost?

AS THE DAY waned and the light in the RV dimmed, Tucker sat in contemplation, staring out the window at the sprawling landscape. He had taken a radical turn, charting a new course for his tenure on the Supreme Court. It was a path fraught with uncertainty and controversy, but for Tucker, it was a path towards establishing his own identity, separate and distinct from the towering figure of Justice Timo.

PART III

UNCONVENTIONAL
JUSTICE

9

THE BILLIONAIRES' JUDGE

The morning was crisp and clear, with a hint of autumn in the air. Justice Cedric Tucker, sitting at his desk in the RV, was reviewing a thick file, its contents reflecting the sunlight streaming through the window.

This file was different – it wasn't a case file or a legal brief, but a collection of correspondences, invitations, and subtle reminders of his connections to some of the nation's most influential billionaires.

TUCKER HAD ALWAYS WANTED to move into the elite circles. Thankfully, his position on the Supreme Court had elevated him to new heights. He was now a coveted guest at private galas, a discreet consultant in high-powered backrooms, and a friend to those who wielded their wealth as a form of silent governance.

This proximity to power had its benefits, but it also brought with it a complex web of expectations and unspoken agreements.

.   .   .

As HE SIFTED through the invitations – each representing a relationship that blurred the lines between personal connection and professional obligation – Tucker was acutely aware of the perception this might create.

To his colleagues and his closet friends, these relationships painted him as the 'Billionaires' Judge,' a title that suggested bias and preferential treatment.

TUCKER'S THOUGHTS were interrupted by a knock on the RV door. It was his wife, Jinny, carrying a fresh batch of correspondence and a worried look. "More invitations, Justice Tucker. Should we go together?"

THE WALDEN ESTATE event was a prime example of Tucker's entanglements. Hosted by a renowned industrial magnate, the event was to be a gathering of the country's most influential figures.

Tucker's presence there, while not unusual for a person of his stature, could raise questions about his impartiality in upcoming cases related to industrial regulations.

HE PONDERED over the right course of action. Declining the invitation could strain a valuable connection, but attending could fuel further allegations of bias. It was a delicate balance, one that Tucker had been managing since his ascent to the Supreme Court.

.   .   .

As he made his decision to attend, rationalizing it as a mere social obligation, Tucker couldn't help but feel a tinge of discomfort.

He had always pretended to be able to navigate these complex social waters, but the increasing scrutiny was starting to weigh heavily on him.

Later that evening, as Tucker prepared for the event, he looked at himself in the mirror. He had come a long way from his humble beginnings in Georgia, rising to the pinnacle of legal authority.

Yet, at this moment, he couldn't shake off the feeling that each step he took in these elite circles was a step away from the principles he once held dear.

As he stepped out of the RV, dressed impeccably for the evening, Tucker was a picture of success and power. But beneath the surface, there was a growing sense of unease, a nagging question about the true cost of his ascent to the top of the legal world.

10

WHISPERS IN THE CORRIDORS

Justice Cedric Tucker's recent decisions and his conspicuous presence at high-profile social events with the country's elite had not gone unnoticed. Within the marbled halls of the Supreme Court and beyond, whispers about his conduct were becoming increasingly common.

IT WAS a typical morning in the Supreme Court, and while the justices convened to discuss their docket, an undercurrent of tension ran through the air. Tucker, ever perceptive, could sense the shift in dynamics.

His colleagues, once open and engaging, now offered only polite smiles and brief nods. The camaraderie that had once defined their interactions seemed to be eroding, replaced by a guarded caution.

IN THE CLERKS' office, the whispers were more pronounced. Young, idealistic law clerks, who once looked up to Tucker as a maverick and a role model, now huddled in corners, their conversations hushed but intense.

They spoke of Tucker's recent rulings, his apparent coziness with wealthy influencers, and the rumors of preferential treatment.

EVEN IN THE CAFETERIA, where legal aides and staff mingled, the murmur of speculation was palpable. Tucker's name came up frequently, often accompanied by raised eyebrows and skeptical looks.

The term 'Billionaires' Judge' had taken on a life of its own, becoming a regular part of whispered gossip.

AMIDST THIS GROWING cloud of suspicion, Tucker walked the halls with his head held high, but the weight of the unspoken words hung heavily around him.

He knew the power of perception, especially in the hallowed realm of the Supreme Court. Reputation was everything, and once tainted, it was a Herculean task to restore it.

ONE AFTERNOON, Tucker's former clerk and confidante on a lower court, Judge Helen Mireles, approached him. "Cedric, there are rumors," she said, her voice tinged with concern. "Rumors that could tarnish not just your reputation, but the integrity of this institution."

TUCKER LISTENED, his expression stoic, but inside, he wrestled with a turmoil of emotions. He had always known that his path would be fraught with challenges, but he had not anticipated the speed and ferocity with which doubt and suspicion could spread.

As HE LAY in his RV that night, miles away from the whispers but not their reach, Tucker reflected on the day's events. The solitude that once brought him clarity now echoed with the voices of his detractors.

The whispers in the corridors had grown louder, morphing into a chorus of doubt that questioned his judgment, his ethics, and his legacy.

IN THE STILLNESS of the night, Justice Tucker understood that the road ahead would be more challenging than he had ever imagined. The battles he would have to fight would not just be legal or ideological, but also against the perceptions that threatened to define him.

The whispers in the corridors, once mere background noise, had become a clarion call for Tucker to confront the growing scrutiny and to defend the integrity of his position and his decisions.

11

THE PRESS TAKES NOTICE

J ustice Cedric Tucker, comfortably ensconced in his RV, chuckled dryly as he leafed through the morning's newspapers. The headlines were sensational, the kind that sold copies and fueled gossip.

"Justice Tucker: Puppet of the Rich?" one read, a bold, almost comedic accusation that would have made Tucker laugh if it weren't so personally targeting.

IN A DRAMATIC TURN OF EVENTS, the media had caught wind of Tucker's lavish escapades and questionable associations with some of the nation's wealthiest figures.

Reporters, always hungry for a scandal, had started piecing together a narrative that painted Tucker as a justice whose gavel was swayed by the rustle of banknotes.

TUCKER FOUND the entire situation absurdly amusing. The thought of giving an interview to clarify his position was laughable. As a Supreme Court Justice and a master of legal manipulation, he knew better than to walk into the lion's den of media scrutiny.

His strategy was avoidance, a dance of denial and deflection he had perfected over the years.

THE RUMORS of Tucker taking bribes were whispered in hushed tones, but they had started to take on a life of their own. Each lavish party he attended, every private jet he boarded, added another thread to the web of deceit he was entangled in.

But Tucker, ever the legal Houdini, managed to wriggle out of these accusations with a mix of charm and calculated ambiguity.

IN THE SUPREME COURT, the atmosphere was electric with unspoken questions. His colleagues, the other justices, were becoming increasingly wary of Tucker's extrajudicial activities.

They maintained a veneer of professionalism in the courtroom, but behind closed doors, their discussions were laced with concern and disapproval.

TUCKER'S LAW CLERKS, a group of bright-eyed legal prodigies, were in a state of moral conflict. They had come to work at the Supreme Court filled with ideals and reverence for the law, only to find themselves working for a man whose actions were at odds with everything they believed in. T

heir hushed conversations, once filled with legal theories and interpretations, now often veered into debates about ethics and integrity.

．　．　．

MEANWHILE, Tucker, seemingly unfazed by the storm brewing around him, continued his charade. He was a master at weaving tales, each more convincing than the last, portraying himself as a misunderstood crusader for justice, maligned by the press and envied by his peers.

As HE PREPARED for another day, another round of social engagements, and another step in the intricate dance of deceit, Tucker couldn't help but admire the irony of it all.

Here he was, a Supreme Court Justice, sworn to uphold the law, yet playing a high-stakes game of smoke and mirrors. It was a game he had become adept at, a game he found thrilling, and, in his most honest moments, a game he knew he couldn't keep playing forever.

IN THE WORLD of justice Tucker had created, the lines between truth and lies, right and wrong, were blurred, and he was the ringmaster, orchestrating each move with the flair of a seasoned performer.

But as the press closed in, and the whispers turned into roars, Tucker knew the final act was approaching, and the curtain could come crashing down at any moment.

12

LEGACY AT STAKE

The early morning light in Justice Cedric Tucker's RV revealed him surrounded by a fortress of legal tomes, but his focus was elsewhere. The headlines, which once seemed amusing in their audacity, were starting to echo the uncomfortable truth of his situation.

With each passing day, the narrative being spun by the media was painting a picture of Tucker that was becoming increasingly difficult to dismiss as mere sensationalism.

THE 'BILLIONAIRES' Judge', as he was now dubbed, was no longer a figure of towering legal intellect, but rather, a caricature in a farcical play of justice.

The irony of it all was not lost on Tucker. The same media he had skillfully evaded and manipulated was slowly turning into his relentless adversary, unraveling the threads of his carefully woven legacy.

. . .

WITHIN THE HALLOWED halls of the Supreme Court, the air was thick with unspoken tension. His fellow justices, once allies and intellectual sparring partners, now regarded him with a mixture of skepticism and wariness.

The usual banter that marked their private gatherings had given way to a strained politeness, a clear sign that Tucker's actions had started to erode the trust and camaraderie essential to their collective work.

THE WHISPERS HAD GROWN LOUDER, not just among the staff and clerks, but in the wider legal community. Rumors of Tucker's alleged improprieties, his extravagant lifestyle, and his questionable associations were now common fodder for discussion at legal conferences and dinners.

The once-revered Justice was slowly becoming an example of how power and influence could taint even the most esteemed legal minds.

TUCKER'S LAW CLERKS, bright young minds who had once viewed their roles as a prestigious stepping stone, now found themselves questioning their career choices. The moral quandary of working for a justice whose principles seemed increasingly at odds with the ideals of the law was a heavy burden to bear.

Their disillusionment was a mirror to Tucker's own internal conflict, though he was loath to admit it.

IN THE SOLITUDE of his RV, Tucker found himself grappling with the reality of his situation. The legacy he had envisioned – one of bold legal strides and revered judicial authority – was crumbling around him.

Each headline, each whispered rumor, each skeptical glance from a colleague, was a reminder of the precariousness of his position.

As HE PREPARED for another day, another round of hearings, and another bout with his own conscience, Tucker realized that the path he had chosen was leading him to an inevitable reckoning.

The charm and wit that had once been his allies were now insufficient shields against the growing storm.

IN A MOMENT OF RARE INTROSPECTION, Tucker acknowledged the irony of his predicament. He had ascended to the highest court in the land, only to find himself ensnared in a web of his own making.

The legacy he had fought so hard to build was at stake, and the battle to save it was becoming increasingly daunting.

As THE SUN ROSE HIGHER, casting a warm glow over the piles of legal work that awaited him, Justice Cedric Tucker knew that the day ahead would be yet another chapter in the unfolding drama of his career – a drama that was edging ever closer to its climax.

PART IV

THE UNRAVELING

13

THE UNBEARABLE LIGHTNESS OF BEING TUCKER

J ustice Cedric Tucker, nestled in the eclectic chaos of his RV, was poring over what could be described as the legal world's latest tragicomedy.

"If this is where the bar is set for emotional distress, I'm an ocean of untapped lawsuits," Tucker chuckled to himself, scribbling a note in the margins of the case file.

HIS AMUSEMENT WAS ABRUPTLY CUT short by a phone call. It was from his assistant, her voice tight with urgency. "Justice Tucker, Chief Justice Reynolds requests your presence immediately."

Tucker's eyebrow arched in intrigue. Chief Justice Ron Reynolds, known for his cautious, often indecisive leadership, rarely demanded anything with such immediacy.

IN CHIEF JUSTICE REYNOLDS' grand, meticulously organized office, Tucker braced himself for a lecture steeped in legal decorum and veiled admonishments.

Reynolds, ever the diplomatic figurehead, was visibly uncomfortable. He cleared his throat, attempting to channel the stern authority of his predecessors, though falling notably short.

"JUSTICE TUCKER, we find ourselves in... troubled waters," Reynolds began, his voice betraying a hint of reluctance. "Your recent... endeavors have stirred quite the pot. We must consider the Court's reputation. We have no choice but to introduce an ethics code of our own."

TUCKER NODDED SAGELY, feigning a gravity he didn't feel. The irony of the situation was too delicious to ignore. Here was Reynolds, a Chief Justice who navigated controversy like a leaf in a storm, always bending to the strongest wind, now trying to anchor the flamboyant Tucker.

"I UNDERSTAND, CHIEF," Tucker replied with a carefully measured tone. "The Court's dignity is paramount." His words were the epitome of judicial solemnity, but his mind was far from solemn.

AS HE LEFT REYNOLDS' office, Tucker mused over the Chief Justice's predicament. Reynolds, in his quest to be the steady hand guiding the Court, often found himself playing to the tune of the more assertive justices.

Now, faced with Tucker's growing notoriety, Reynolds was trying to steer the ship away from turbulent waters, much like a sick captain negotiating a storm with a rudder made of good intentions.

BACK IN HIS RV, Tucker returned to the bizarre zoo case. The absurdity of it provided a welcome respite from the gravity of his meeting with Reynolds. "If only the Chief is half as good as his predecessors," Tucker thought, a wry smile playing on his lips.

AS HE DRAFTED HIS OPINION, Tucker couldn't help but draw parallels between the case and his current predicament. Both were, in their essence, about overstepping boundaries – the Plaintiff with his mind, and Tucker with his judicial discretion.

YET, unlike the psychic plaintiff, Tucker had no intention of backing down. Reynolds' veiled request for restraint had fallen on deaf ears.

Tucker was no Fortas, ready to resign at the first hint of controversy. He was a different breed, one without shame or, seemingly, limits.

THAT NIGHT, as Tucker penned his opinion under the soft glow of his desk lamp, the RV felt like a cocoon, shielding him from the storm brewing outside.

In his judicial cocoon, Tucker was untouchable – a law unto himself, dancing on the fine line between legal brilliance and audacious defiance.

14

SHADOWS OF DOUBT

Justice Cedric Tucker sat in his RV, his usual fortress of solitude, now feeling more like the eye of a storm. Around him, the walls of his legal bastion seemed to close in, each newspaper headline, each whispered rumor adding to the pressure.

The latest news had hit him like a ton of bricks: an official investigation by the Senate was underway, probing into his alleged unethical conduct.

THE INVESTIGATION, initiated by a coalition of concerned legal scholars and former judges, was a direct response to the growing unease about Tucker's activities both inside and outside the courtroom.

The inquiry aimed to shed light on Tucker's connections with influential billionaires and their potential impact on his judicial decisions.

. . .

T UCKER, who had always managed to dance around accusations with the grace of a seasoned politician, found himself in unfamiliar territory.

The shadows of doubt were no longer just whispers in the corridors of the Supreme Court or sensational headlines; they were taking form in the shape of legal inquiries and demands for transparency.

H E THOUGHT back to the conversation with Chief Justice Reynolds, whose warnings now seemed almost prophetic. Reynolds, for all his shortcomings, had sensed the brewing trouble, a storm that Tucker had underestimated.

"They wouldn't be able to find anything. I am too important to the Republicans," he was willing to lie to himself though.

A S HE SAT PONDERING his next move, Tucker's phone rang. It was his lawyer, a man more accustomed to dealing with mundane legal matters than navigating the treacherous waters of a judicial investigation.

"Cedric, this is serious. They're digging deep, and they're asking for everything – emails, phone records, travel logs," his lawyer briefed him, the concern in his voice unmistakable.

T UCKER RESPONDED with a nonchalant wave of his hand, although his lawyer couldn't see it. "Let them look. They won't find anything I can't handle," he replied, his voice a mixture of bravado and denial.

· · ·

BUT DEEP DOWN, Tucker knew this was different. The investigation wasn't just a probe into a single dubious decision or a questionable remark; it was a comprehensive inquiry into his entire career on the bench. It was as if the very foundations of his judicial life were being scrutinized, every stone turned, every skeleton threatened with exposure.

THE IRONY of the situation was not lost on him. Here he was, a Supreme Court Justice, a paragon of legal virtue in the public eye, now the subject of an investigation that could potentially undo everything he had worked for.

The once-clear lines between his personal and professional life, lines he had so skillfully blurred to his advantage, were now the very thing that ensnared him.

AS DUSK FELL, Tucker sat alone in the dimming light, surrounded by the trappings of his judicial life. The RV, once a symbol of his freedom and independence, now felt like a gilded cage.

The investigation, with its unyielding scrutiny, cast long shadows of doubt over Tucker's legacy – shadows that threatened to engulf him in a darkness of his own making

15

THE TEFLON JUSTICE

Justice Cedric Tucker reclined in his RV, surrounded by the trappings of his recent controversies – stacks of legal documents, swirling media reports, and the ever-looming shadow of the ongoing investigation.

With a wry smile, he muttered to himself, "The First Amendment is always on my side, no matter what my side is."

THIS WAS Tucker's way of shrugging off the latest development: a probe by Congress into his conduct. The inquiry, meant to be a thorough examination, was faltering.

The congressional GOP, many of whom were beneficiaries of Tucker's billionaire friends, resisted the probe at every turn. These friends, who once graced the pages of society columns, were now cited in legal arguments, trying to evade scrutiny by wielding their influence and citing a concoction of legal loopholes and privileges.

. . .

TUCKER FOUND the whole situation absurdly amusing. He had always prided himself on being untouchable – the Teflon Justice, where accusations and suspicions never seemed to stick.

Now, watching the powerful machinations at play to shield him, he felt a sense of invincibility. It was as though he was the protagonist in a farcical drama, where the lines between legality and ethics were blurred beyond recognition.

THE INVESTIGATION, though thorough in its intent, was turning into a circus of legal technicalities. Tucker's billionaire friends were mounting a defense that was as robust as it was ridiculous, citing freedom of speech, legal privileges, and a myriad of other constitutional protections to shield their dealings with the Justice.

AS TUCKER PONDERED over his next move, his phone rang. It was Jinny, her voice a mix of concern and naivety. "Cedric, this all seems so... messy. Would I get into trouble as well?"

TUCKER CHUCKLED at the simplicity of her view. "Darling, it's politics and law intertwined. It's never that simple. But don't you worry, I've always landed on my feet. I will have you covered"

IN HIS HEART, though, Tucker knew that this situation was different. The allegations were sticking, slowly eroding the Teflon coating he had so carefully applied over the years.

For the first time, he felt the tinge of vulnerability, a crack in his armor that he couldn't easily mend.

THAT NIGHT, as Tucker drafted responses to the latest round of inquiries, he couldn't help but marvel at the irony of it all. He had spent his career bending the law to his will, only to find himself entangled in a legal web of his own making.

The First Amendment, his supposed shield, was now being wielded against him in a battle of wits and wills.

AS HE TURNED off the lights, preparing for a restless night, Tucker realized that his legacy was no longer in his hands. It was being shaped by the very forces he had once manipulated with ease.

The Teflon Justice, for all his cunning and wit, was facing the ultimate test – a battle not in the courtroom, but in the court of public opinion and the hallowed halls of Congress. And in this battle, the rules were constantly changing, and the stakes were higher than ever.

16

THE COURT OF ABSURD OPINIONS

J ustice Cedric Tucker, once the lion of the legal world, now found himself in the unenviable position of being the court jester. As he sat in his RV – his mobile throne room turned clown car – he couldn't help but chuckle at the latest headline:

"Justice Tucker – From Bench to Circus?" It seemed his esteemed career was now a prime-time comedy show, and he was the unwitting star.

THE MEDIA FRENZY had reached new heights of absurdity, with pundits and armchair legal experts dissecting Tucker's every move and decision.

Each analysis was more ludicrous than the last, turning complex legal issues into fodder for late-night talk show jokes. "Next, they'll say I'm in cahoots with extraterrestrials to manipulate the legal system," Tucker mused, sipping his morning coffee with a smirk.

. . .

AMIDST THIS FARCE, the Supreme Court was in turmoil. The once-stately conferences had devolved into something resembling a dysfunctional family dinner.

Justices tiptoed around Tucker, treating him like a grenade that could go off at any moment.

Chief Justice Reynolds, in his attempts to maintain decorum, often ended up stammering through his words, like a nervous host trying to avoid a scene.

TUCKER, for his part, relished the chaos. He strode into the courtroom with the swagger of a man who had nothing to lose, tossing out witty quips and provocative comments that left his colleagues gaping. His new mantra seemed to be, "If I'm going down, I'm doing it in style."

THE CLERKS AND JUNIOR STAFF, who once revered the Supreme Court as a temple of justice, were now betting on how long it would take for

Tucker to completely derail a session. They whispered and snickered behind legal briefs, passing around caricatures of Tucker drawn on the margins of memos.

MEANWHILE, the investigation continued to unfold in a tragicomic spectacle. Tucker's billionaire friends, with their armies of lawyers, spun webs of legal jargon so dense, they seemed to be creating their own alternate reality.

The congressional probe, rather than being an inquiry, was more akin to a puppet show, with Tucker's allies and supporters pulling the strings from behind the curtain.

· · ·

IN THE MIDST of this legal circus, Tucker received a call from Jinny.

"Cedric, you're on every channel! They're making a mockery of everything. Can't you do something for me?" she pleaded, her voice a mix of frustration and despair.

TUCKER LAUGHED HEARTILY. "My dear, when life gives you lemons, juggle them on national television. If I'm the star of this absurd show, I might as well give a performance to remember."

AS HE ENDED THE CALL, Tucker looked around his RV, once a symbol of freedom and independence, now a backstage room for the greatest show on earth.

With a sigh, he turned his attention to his work, ready to pen another opinion that would no doubt add fuel to the comedic fire burning around him.

IN THE COURT OF ABSURD OPINIONS, Justice Cedric Tucker reigned supreme, his gavel a scepter of satire, his robes the costume of a tragic hero in a play where every act was more ridiculous than the last. The show, it seemed, was far from over.

17

LAST LUXURY TRIP

J ustice Cedric Tucker's RV, once a beacon of judicial independence, had transformed into a bizarre social club on wheels. Today, it was hosting an unusual guest – one of Tucker's billionaire friends, Vincent Harrow, known for his lavish lifestyle and a knack for staying just on the right side of legal controversies.

As THE RV trundled along a scenic route, the two old friends were engrossed in a conversation that would have seemed surreal to any outsider.

They were debating the merits of various luxury hotels, comparing the opulence of private yachts, and reminiscing about extravagant parties in exotic locales.

"NEXT TIME, Cedric, we must choose between the penthouse suite at my Three Seasons or my private island. The jet's ready whenever you are," Harrow mused, swirling a glass of expensive scotch.

. . .

TUCKER, despite the looming clouds of his legal troubles, reveled in the conversation. "Ah, Vincent, the decisions we must make. It's a tough life, but someone's got to live it," he replied with a hearty laugh, clinking his glass with Harrow's.

BUT BENEATH THE veneer of luxury and nonchalance, a different drama was unfolding.

Harrow, like many of Tucker's affluent associates, was beginning to feel the heat from Tucker's increasingly precarious position. The media scrutiny and the ongoing investigation were casting a wide net, and Harrow was wary of being caught in the backlash.

AS THE RV rolled into the sunset, Harrow's jovial facade began to crack. "Cedric, are you sure you're... handling things well?

This investigation could get ugly for all of us," he said, his tone laced with a concern that was more for himself than for Tucker.

TUCKER, sensing the shift in Harrow's demeanor, masked his own rising sense of isolation with bravado. "Vincent, my dear friend, worry not. I've danced with wolves fiercer than these investigators. I'll come out of this unscathed, as always."

. . .

BUT HARROW WAS NOT CONVINCED. The Tucker he saw now was a far cry from the shrewd, untouchable Justice he had known. This Tucker was more a desperate showman, clinging to the remnants of his power and influence.

The realization that Tucker might no longer be the shield against legal repercussions, but rather the magnet attracting them, was dawning on Harrow.

THE EVENING ENDED with a lavish dinner at a secluded five-star restaurant, but the opulence felt hollow. Harrow, under the guise of scheduling conflicts, excused himself from future engagements, a subtle yet clear sign of distancing.

AS TUCKER RETURNED to his RV, alone, he couldn't shake off a sense of abandonment. The laughter and chatter of the evening echoed mockingly in the silence.

His friends, the high-flying socialites and power brokers, were starting to desert him. The realization stung, not just because of the personal betrayal but because it signaled the crumbling of the world he had built.

IN THE SOLITUDE of his RV, Justice Cedric Tucker faced a truth he had long evaded – his empire of influence was fading, and with it, the identity he had crafted for himself.

The road ahead was uncertain, and for the first time, Tucker felt the pangs of doubt about the journey he had chosen.

PART V
THE FALL

18

TWO-THIRD MAJORITY

I n the dim light of his RV, Justice Cedric Tucker sat, a solitary figure amidst a sea of legal briefs and newspapers. The news playing in the background was a cacophony of political upheaval; President Broden had secured a second term, this time with a Senate majority large enough to entertain the unthinkable – the impeachment of a Supreme Court Justice.

Tucker, with his swirl of controversies and the persistent bribery rumors that dated back to Broden's first term, was squarely in the crosshairs.

THE RELATIONSHIP between Tucker and President Broden had always been complex. Broden, overseeing Martha Thiel's hearing in a parallel to Tucker's own confirmation, had never truly favored Tucker.

It was more a case of political incapacity that had allowed Tucker's appointment to slip through during Broden's initial term.

Now, with a stronger mandate, Broden's administration seemed poised to correct that oversight.

TUCKER, now in his 70s, watched the unfolding drama with a mix of defiance and resignation. The rumors of bribery, once mere whispers, had grown into a chorus calling for accountability.

The political landscape had shifted, and Tucker, once untouchable, found himself vulnerable to the whims of a Senate baying for justice.

INITIALLY, Tucker had scoffed at the idea of resigning. His mind, sharp as ever, refused to entertain the notion of bowing out under pressure.

However, recent events had started to chip away at his resolve. His memory wasn't as reliable as it once was, a creeping fog that reminded him uncomfortably of Justice Douglas' latter days.

Briefs and arguments that he would have once dissected with ease now took longer to comprehend, their complexities unraveling slower in his mind.

ADDING to his woes was the strain in his personal life. Jinny, his wife, had become distant, her affections cooling into a polite indifference that was more cutting than outright hostility.

Tucker had caught whispers of her indiscretions, though he never confronted her. In his heart, he knew their marriage was unraveling, much like his career.

· · ·

As Tucker sat in contemplation, the weight of his situation became increasingly clear. His health, both mental and physical, was declining.

The political tides had turned against him, and the support he had once taken for granted was slipping away. The thought of being impeached, of leaving the bench in disgrace, was anathema to him.

In a rare moment of clarity, Tucker realized that his options were limited. Resigning would be a blow to his pride, but it would allow him to maintain some control over his narrative, to leave on his own terms rather than being ousted in a humiliating spectacle.

With a heavy heart, Tucker began drafting his letter of resignation. The words were difficult to come by, each sentence a reminder of the end of a once-stellar career.

As he wrote, he couldn't help but reflect on the irony of it all - the once-great Justice Tucker, brought down not just by external forces, but by the slow betrayal of his own body and heart.

The political winds had shifted, and with them, the fate of Justice Cedric Tucker. What lay ahead was uncertain, but for the first time in a long while, Tucker felt the weight of his own vulnerability.

In the quiet of his RV, a chapter was closing, and the legacy of one of the most controversial figures in the American judiciary was drawing to an unceremonious end.

19

THE GRAND IMPEACHMENT

The sun had barely risen, casting a pale light over Justice Cedric Tucker's RV, now parked in a secluded area far from the prying eyes of the media and the public.

Inside, Tucker sat at his makeshift desk, surrounded by the remnants of his storied career – legal books, newspaper clippings, and his resignation letter, a document that symbolized his capitulation to the inevitable.

THE NEWS of Tucker's impending resignation had sent shockwaves through the political and legal realms. It was a victory for the liberals, a tragedy for the conservatives, and a source of relentless speculation for all.

DESPITE HIS DECISION TO RESIGN, the wheels of justice continued to turn, and the impeachment process, already set in motion, was gaining momentum.

· · ·

TUCKER, once a master of legal strategy, found himself on the defensive, a role he was unaccustomed to and ill-prepared for.

The Senate, now with a robust Democratic majority under President Broden's second term, was moving forward with the impeachment proceedings, undeterred by Tucker's decision to step down.

The hearings, broadcast live and dissected by pundits across the nation, were less about seeking truth and more about political theater – a spectacle where Tucker was both the star and the scapegoat.

THE IRONY of the situation was not lost on him; the very people who had once lauded his judicial acumen were now questioning his integrity and fitness to serve.

THE TESTIMONIES WERE a mix of factual recounting and dramatic storytelling, painting Tucker as a man who had let his power and influence cloud his judgment.

Witnesses, ranging from legal experts to former clerks, took the stand, each adding their narrative to the growing case against him.

IN A PARTICULARLY POIGNANT MOMENT, a former clerk, once a bright-eyed believer in Tucker's brand of justice, spoke of disillusionment and moral conflict.

"I admired Justice Tucker," the young lawyer said, pausing to compose himself. "But I came to realize that the law, in his hands, was not about justice but about power."

. . .

TUCKER, watching the testimony, felt a pang of something he couldn't quite identify – regret, perhaps, or a mournful acknowledgment of the impact of his actions on those who had once looked up to him.

AS THE DAY of the final vote neared, Tucker's sense of isolation deepened. The RV, once a symbol of his freedom and independence, now felt like a solitary confinement cell, a place where he awaited the final judgment of his peers.

THE DAY of the vote arrived, and Tucker watched with a resigned detachment. The outcome was a foregone conclusion; the Senate, with its overwhelming Democratic majority, had the numbers to impeach him.

The vote was swift, and the verdict was as expected – Tucker was to be impeached, a sad day in the history of the Supreme Court.

AS THE GAVEL CAME DOWN, marking the end of the proceedings, Tucker turned off the television. The storm had passed, leaving in its wake the remnants of a career that had once been the envy of the legal world.

In the quiet aftermath, Justice Cedric Tucker sat alone, contemplating the end of an era – his era – and the uncertain path that lay ahead.

20

PAYING THE PRICE

I n the waning light of dusk, Justice Cedric Tucker sat alone in his RV, parked on the outskirts of a forgotten forest. The world outside was a blur, its noises distant and muffled, as if he were submerged in a deep, somber sea.

The RV, once a vessel of freedom and escape, now felt like a floating tomb, carrying the remnants of a once-great legacy.

TUCKER, his silhouette barely discernible in the dimming light, was a picture of Shakespearean tragedy. His fall from grace was not just a legal defeat; it was the crumbling of a colossus, a man who once held the law in the palm of his hand, now reduced to a mere mortal, grappling with his own mortality and relevance.

THE IMPEACHMENT, a public spectacle that had stripped him of his judicial robes, echoed the dramatic downfalls of history's most tragic figures. Tucker's life had become an ironic play of hubris and nemesis, where his greatest strengths had turned into his most fatal flaws.

THE NEWSPAPERS, strewn across the table, bore headlines that spoke of his demise, but Tucker's eyes were fixed on the window, gazing out at the twilight sky.

The fading light seemed to mirror his own journey – the brilliant blaze of his career now giving way to the inevitable darkness.

THE LONELINESS WAS PALPABLE. His friends, once numerous and influential, had vanished like shadows at dawn, leaving Tucker to face his twilight alone.

Jinny, too, was absent, her love and loyalty lost in the labyrinth of Tucker's ambition and pride. The silence of the RV was a stark contrast to the laughter and lively debates it once housed, a reminder of the isolation that power often brings.

AS THE LAST vestiges of light disappeared, Tucker's mind wandered through the memories of his past – the victories, the accolades, and the sense of invincibility. Each memory was tinged with a bitter realization that his downfall was of his own making, a tragic flaw that had sealed his fate.

IN THE QUIET of the night, Tucker poured himself a drink, the liquid amber a small comfort in his solitary confinement. He raised the glass, a toast to the ghosts of his past, to the dreams that had turned to dust.

"To justice," he whispered, his voice a hollow echo in the vast emptiness of his RV.

THE NIGHT DEEPENED, and Tucker sat there, a fallen titan, engulfed in the tragic twilight of his life. The glory and power he had once wielded were now just whispers in the wind, tales to be told in the annals of judicial history.

In the solitude of his mobile sanctuary, Cedric Tucker faced the end of his era – not with the defiance of old, but with the tragic acceptance of a man who had flown too close to the sun and had been scorched by its flames.

21

THE BROKEN MAN

In the grand office of the Attorney General of a prominent red state, Alex Mercer, once a bright-eyed law clerk under Justice Cedric Tucker, gazed out the window at the bustling city below.

The news of Tucker's tragic downfall had reverberated through the legal community, leaving a profound impact on those who had once worked closely with the fallen titan.

MERCER, now established in a role that wielded significant influence, reflected on Tucker's legacy. The office was quiet, the only sound being the gentle hum of the city.

On Mercer's desk lay a photograph taken years ago, showing a younger version of Mercer alongside Justice Tucker, both smiling, full of confidence and ambition.

AS MERCER PONDERED, there was a sense of melancholy, a realization that Tucker's downfall was not just personal but a loss to the conservative legal world.

"There will never be another conservative justice like him," Mercer thought, a statement filled with both admiration and regret.

HOWEVER, Mercer's reflections were tinged with a deeper understanding, one that extended beyond political affiliations and legal ideologies. Tucker's story was a stark reminder of the importance of moral character in the selection of justices.

It wasn't just about appointing individuals who championed a particular legal philosophy or political stance; it was about ensuring that those who were entrusted with upholding the law embodied the principles of integrity, fairness, and ethical conduct.

TUCKER, for all his brilliance and judicial acumen, had been flawed in ways that went to the core of these values. His fall from grace underscored the perils of prioritizing ideology over character, of placing legal prowess above ethical standards.

It was a lesson that Mercer, and indeed the legal community at large, could not afford to ignore.

IN THE SOLITUDE of the office, Mercer made a silent vow – to uphold the law with the integrity that the role demanded, to remember that the power vested in legal positions was a trust to be honored, not a privilege to be exploited.

Mercer understood that the legal landscape needed champions who were not only intellectually competent but morally sound, individuals who could carry the mantle of justice with dignity and honor.

As the day drew to a close, Mercer turned off the lights and stepped out of the office. The photograph of Tucker was left on the desk, a relic of a bygone era and a reminder of the lessons learned from a once-great jurist's tragic tale.

In the corridors of power and the halls of justice, the story of Cedric Tucker would be recounted for generations to come – not just as a cautionary tale of a fallen titan but as a profound lesson in the importance of character in the guardians of the law.

For in the end, the true legacy of a justice lay not in the legal battles won or the ideologies championed, but in the moral integrity with which they served the law and the people it was meant to protect.

www.ingramcontent.com/pod-product-compliance
Lightning Source LLC
Chambersburg PA
CBHW050508290526
45786CB00006B/2490